Time in Eternity

Tom Merrill

ANCIENT CYPRESS PRESS
Fort Lauderdale

Ancient Cypress Press
Fort Lauderdale
Florida, USA
www.ancientcypresspress.com

Copyright © 2013 Ancient Cypress Press
Ancient Cypress Press® is a registered trademark.

All rights reserved—no part of this book may be reproduced in any form without permission in writing from the publisher, except by a reviewer who wishes to quote brief passages in connection with a review in a magazine or newspaper.

ISBN: 978-0-9889648-2-2

Cover illustration: "Eternity," by Mary Rae

Acknowledgments

With special thanks to the first publishers of the poems listed:

The Lyric: ……. "I Do Not See," "Return," " Infiltration," "I Had of Love," "Of Modern Mysteries," "Forever Lacking," "Undying Love," "I Watched," "Seeing," "Unwithered," "Novenas," "Come Lord and Lift," "For a Stricken Innocent," "Prayer," "Mother of Joy, of Sorrows," "Then to Thee Gladly," "Regardless," "Scattered Ashes," "Huit Clos," "Departure," "In the Stillness of Many," "Song of the Alley Cat," "Then Pines," "Blessing the Cup," "Companions," "Adventure Beckons," "A Minor Croak," "After the Hurricane," "Summer Yardwork," "Love Came a Second Time," "Brighter Are All," "Into the Winter Clad," "Once," "By Land or By Sea," "Outlaw's Retreat"

The Hypertexts: ……. "Though Sorrow Mock," "A Loan and a Lease," "Orbiting a Potentially Dead Star," "In God We Trust," "That Old-Time Religion," "The Rock of the Redeemer," "The Immortal Path," "Love's Legacy," "Heeding the Prophet," "The Marionette Show," "Letting in the Draft," "On the Urgency of Replenishing the Workforce," "A Brief Alarm," "Chapeau Bouquet," "A Demurral," "Quoth the Raven from the Ballroom Bar," "Bypassing the Mill," "Frequent Flyer Program," "Shock Therapy," "Death in Life," "Diluvian Meditation," "On a Proposed New Course," "Officially Speaking," "An Ideal Substitution," "Madame LaBouche," "A Hoot for the Labor League," "US in Them," "Cell Theory," "Palmistry in Paradise," "Reactionary Phase," "Square Times Blues," "Preparing for the Pageant," "Advice for Winston," "Between Frosts,"

"Personal Exemption," "Consolation for the Disenchanted," "Canadian Club vs. Catechism Class," "Going with the Flow," "Auscultation"

Orphic Lute: .... "Time in Eternity," "I Threw off Love," "How Only Cold," "Sad Dreamer to His Love," "Tomorrow Some New Star," "Urban Fare," "Pronounced and Deep," "Who Long Kept Hid"

The Archer: .... "Excerpt from Hamlet's Diary," "Such Things Must Draw"

Midwest Poetry Review: .... "ee cummings"

Contents

I Do Not See	15
Return	16
Though Sorrow Mock	17
Infiltration	18
Who Long Kept Hid	19
I Had of Love	20
Of Modern Mysteries	21
A Loan and a Lease	22
Forever Lacking	23
Time in Eternity	24
Undying Love	25
I Watched	26
I Threw Off Love	27
Orbiting a Potentially Dead Star	28
Seeing	29
Unwithered	30
How Only Cold	31
Sad Dreamer to His Love	32
Novenas	33
Come Lord and Lift	34
For a Stricken Innocent	35
Prayer	36
Mother of Joy, of Sorrows	37
Then to Thee Gladly	38
In God We Trust	39
That Old-Time Religion	40

The Rock of the Redeemer	41
The Immortal Path	42
Love's Legacy	43
Heeding the Prophet	44
The Marionette Show	45
Letting in the Draft	46
Regardless	47
On the Urgency of Replenishing the Workforce	48
A Brief Alarm	49
Chapeau Bouquet	50
A Demurral	51
Quoth the Raven from the Ballroom Bar	52
Bypassing the Mill	54
Frequent Flyer Program	55
Scattered Ashes	56
Shock Therapy	57
Death in Life	58
Huit Clos	59
Diluvian Meditation	60
On a Proposed New Course	61
Officially Speaking	62
Revenge of the Clock	63
Departure	64
An Ideal Substitution	65
Excerpt from Hamlet's Diary	66
In the Stillness of Many	67
Tomorrow Some New Star	68
Madame LaBouche	69

Song of the Alley Cat	70
Urban Fare	71
A Hoot for the Labor League	72
US in Them	73
Cell Theory	74
Palmistry in Paradise	75
Reactionary Phase	76
Square Times Blues	77
Preparing for the Pageant	78
Advice for Winston	79
Between Frosts	80
Then Pines	81
Pronounced and Deep	82
Blessing the Cup	83
Companions	84
Adventure Beckons	85
Personal Exemption	86
ee cummings	87
A Minor Croak	88
After the Hurricane	89
Consolation for the Disenchanted	90
Summer Yardwork	91
Canadian Club vs. Catechism Class	92
Going with the Flow	93
Auscultation	94
Such Things Must Draw	95
Love Came a Second Time	96
Brighter Are All	97

Into the Winter Clad	98
Once	99
By Land or By Sea	100
Outlaw's Retreat	101

Here is a keepsake for two special people,
Beekerson Fleurimond and Tommy Bissonnette,
both resident in Quebec,
who between them inspired five of the poems
that got selected by the publisher for inclusion in this collection;
and here too is a resort for any odd person
to whom any of my language or themes may speak.

Time in Eternity

I Do Not See

I do not see the stars tonight
   Nor wonder if they shine,
For many years have passed since I
   Wished any beauty mine.

I do not seek the flowered wood's
   Unworldly hush and stir,
Nor are there cherished haunts of mind
   As long ago there were.

I find no sail to lull me now
   Away to courts of dream,
And upward from the sod I push
   Blue skies fade out unseen.

Return

When somehow you appeared and took
    This heart not mine to give,
And spring broke out again and gave
    Me every cause to live,

It seemed as if some power had sent
    A spirit to restore
That other Eden that I knew,
    When all was lost before.

Though Sorrow Mock

I shall not give you up for lost,
   Though grief prevail,
   Tears overcome,
   Strength fail;

Though silence join with ash
   To prove all perish;
   Though sorrow mock my hope
   For all I cherish.

Infiltration

Useless though these walls have been
   For keeping out hell's horrors,
Here they stand, against what glides
   With ease through solid borders;

Or stand they must, if seeming no
   More bound to serve than I,
Who know how fiends come drifting in,
   Yet wait love's urgent cry.

Who Long Kept Hid

I prayed to stars, when I was young,
   To lure love where I lay
Lone as a shore that calls a sea
   The tide has turned away.

Love did not come, and oh they seemed
   Indifferent to my cry,
Who long kept hid how love could be
   A kindness to deny.

I Had of Love

I had of love, when it first came,
    A single, lonesome bolt;
It had but one—and I could find
    No living antidote.

And so, I made my cure of hearts
    A cold night wind instead,
And all the sadly brimming stars
    Shone down on our chill bed.

And then I hummed forgotten fields
    A lover's lullaby,
And by the fallen gates of hope,
    We wept, the wind and I.

Of Modern Mysteries

My love is no new poet,
But has a simple tongue;
To love, no use in speaking
Except as to the young.

And whom else should we speak to
If not the one we love?
And so I seldom speak as
If speaking from above.

I do not darkly draw what
I most want understood,
But often say "I love you,"
As bygone poets would.

A Loan and a Lease

He lay so quietly I reached
Over to feel if he was warm;
Hearing no breath, I needed proof
No chill was on that too-still form.
He came without his one-track side,
Just humbly handsome and polite,
And it was good of him to both
Show himself and spend the night.

A switch I got to mute the bells
Stays off or on as I allow,
But at the moment keeps the peace.
My house will not withstand its flaws,
But while my lucky star shines on
I'm hoping to renew the lease.

—for Tommy

Forever Lacking

However well you show the way,
  My brave and ailing child,
By meeting every demon with
  A spirit angel-mild,

Still I go plunging toward regret,
  And cannot learn your art,
Forever lacking strength to bind
  My action to my heart.

Time in Eternity

When you were as an angel in my arms,
Had laid your bare head just below my chin,
Your length pressed up to mine, entrusting charms
My whole youth's starward longing could not win;
With still the murmur of your love in me,
Miracle-tones of all my lifelong hope,
I wished that there might start eternity
And seal forever that sweet envelope;
And as it did, my thoughts are now for you
As every star is blotted by the sun,
And so the sun itself
Has perished too,
And with it, every dream of mine
But one.

Undying Love

My love is any towering pine
   That stands erect as ever,
And shows no sign of having swayed
   Through any purge of weather;

Sure-rooted as the tallest tree
   Beneath a changeful sky,
It stands, as if no storms had struck,
   Nor loves were born to die.

I Watched

I watched love weather, near as you
   The dagger of the word;
Like pharaoh from his throne I watched—
   From love, no cry was heard.

I watched an eye that gazed its gaze,
   I watched lips firmly still;
I watched a valiant mask, as if
   To watch my dagger kill.

And as a helpless cheek betrayed
   The certain hurt within,
I did not stem the tide, but watched
   Blood blossom on the skin.

And when from love a sound rose up
   That rent my heart in two,
I watched—I watched a thing too weak
   To swear its words untrue.

I Threw Off Love

I threw off love the other day,
   The only thing I'd keep;
I flung it at the giver of
   My very peace in sleep;

For so the after-hours revealed,
   One price of my rash sin
Was purchase of a rockbed no
   Sweet dreams could flourish in.

Orbiting a Potentially Dead Star

My heart got hooked again last week,
and today,

full of foreboding,
I'm reading all the signs as grave,

sensing an ominous vacancy,
non-existence as fait accompli,

a savior come and gone like a god
no god can grant eternity.

Two sacred little bottles missing
from my quaint majolica humidor,

a perpetual "sorry, call-limit reached,"
that hopeless head two nights ago

wet on my ceded chest and sobbing
"I curse the day I was born" all seem

to point to those two times before
when he tried to rob the world of treasure,

plunged deep enough for wakelessness,
for being forever out of means

to deflect a mind from helpless orbit
around a single constant care,

from a huge gravitational trap of feeling
bound to a heart no longer there.

Seeing

Seeing that ill must come between
   And neither can be true,
How either you are bound to leave,
   Or I to part from you—

We lose too much to sad regret,
   Too much feel joy as sorrow,
Too little trust in what may keep,
   Too well foresee tomorrow.

Unwithered

Unwithered by all casting out
  My demon drives me yet
Down the dark path that always ends
  In sorrow and regret,

And leaves me to repent again
  My neverending part
In injuring a perfect love,
  And breaking my own heart.

How Only Cold

If to such happiness an end must come,
As ends may swallow all dear hopes and dreams,
And should you vanish, and my heart grow numb
With sorrow, as though yet so soon it seems;
And if the bitterness should long consume
My thoughts of you, who briefly lit the day,
And sun no more return to re-illume
And lift the flower withered in the clay;
Yet memory of a distant atmosphere,
Travail obscure as rock in some dark field,
The glassed-in din's dull pulsing in my ear,
Faint throb of stars, so long astir but sealed,
Recalls a love left even more alone,
How only cold released the ache of stone.

Sad Dreamer to His Love

I sorrow that we cannot have
Sown garden, birdsong, grass and trees—
Sweet things that lend—to others—ease—
Or ample space to mend our lives
Immured against all outside eyes
By riotous rose-hedge, hemlock, fir—
Wherein, a little wilderness were
Our own, were things made different, love;
But do not trouble Him above;
To the ambitious goes the day,
They claim the field, they sow the May;
Poor fancy yields but small return,
Though chance *has,* weighed elseways,
Shared love's concern.

Novenas

After defeat, in grief's most hopeless hours,
With no resort remaining but the void,
The vanquished yet may turn to hidden powers,
Begging protection for a heart destroyed.
As crown or cross perhaps recalls some scene,
Bead by sad bead they may beseech the air,
As though in precincts silent and unseen
Lost angels could be helped by human prayer.

Each may, as if some hearing had begun
In secret parts where all the dead yet live,
Cry out to walls the innocence of one
Whom now no other aid is left to give.
And whether justice anywhere may reign,
None here can prove their witness was in vain.

Come Lord and Lift

Come Lord, and lift the fallen bird
   Abandoned on the ground;
The soul bereft and longing so
   To have the lost be found.

The heart that cries—let it but hear
   Its sweet love answering,
Or out of ether one faint note
   Of living comfort wring.

For a Stricken Innocent

Thy child who cries to me, Lord,
    Finds no relieving art,
But only helpless anguish,
    As with a bursting heart

I gather to me gently
    Joy brittle and too brief;
O take him up as I do,
    O be a gentle thief.

Prayer

O merciful Mother, protect him,
   Who bears so much alone,
My only, and my dearest,
   And guiltless like your own;

My little one, who suffers,
   And needs your comfort now;
O help him, Merciful Mother,
   For I do not know how.

Mother of Joy, of Sorrows

Such innocence as never
    Before on earth had smiled,
You bore, O Holy Mother,
    Then saw your only child,

Your precious joy, your sorrow
    Endure his tragic load,
And watched, as I watch now,
    Through tears, beside the road.

Then to Thee Gladly

O Lord,
   if in the sight of Thee
   is peace, and happiness
   fills all who look
   on Thee;
And where Thou art,
   all troubles
   truly cease, and Thou
    art truly, and as said
    to be;
Then to Thee gladly
   I send forth
   my love—to Thy
    protection, speed
    an ill-used guest;
From sorrow, anguish,
   tears, to aeons of
   that light,
    which but to look upon
    is rest.

(This poem hangs in the musem of
The Cathedral of the Pines in
Rindge, New Hampshire.)

In God We Trust

Absolve yourselves, believe them saved,
Whom hungrily you brought to fare
As chance decrees, and leave to them
The fortune to which you rose heir.
Now theirs shall be the kingdom too,
This one and that, and all they hold,
All marvels present, and as well
Fresh wonders when the flesh turns cold.

All you who by blind pulse renew
The primal blessing cast in heat,
And to a season's course entrust
Frail issue weather can defeat,
Who from flung seed grew anxious too—
Deny earth feeds on them and you.

That Old-Time Religion

*"Now I want you to go out there
and enjoy yourself, and yes, enjoy
your philosophy of life, too."* — John Ashbery,
from "My Philosophy of Life."

Ashbery wishes us good times,
And me, I hope they won't abate.
I want the moments I have now
Never to evaporate.
I've made a niche, and won some thrills
By luck at playing hit or miss—
Enough to keep my outlook rich
And life appearing generous.

Since one now holds a special claim,
I tend desire's lesser leaks
Until that bronze funicular
Returns to run me to the peaks
And sets an eager artist free
To blanch a canvas jauntily.

—pour Beekerson Fleurimond

The Rock of the Redeemer

Each week he orbits back again to mine
Old quarries, prop the faithful, and be swept
Rock-borne from door to door, through days and nights
And on to where revered remains are kept.
Some groomed disciple then will softly keep
Long watch, until the moment when at last
All done with sacrifice, the rock rolled back,
The lamb bursts forth, intent on breaking fast;

So weekly feasts are hastily prepared,
By way of thanks for many feats performed
And toils endured to keep old fans attached—
Some scourging, blood, and other gifts to leaven
The outlook of his flock, which deems the rock
His church stands on, the keystone of their heaven.

*(Author's note: "Rock" is a street name
for a popular illegal substance.)*

The Immortal Path

"The assassin discloses himself,
The force that destroys us is disclosed...
an adventure to be endured
With the politest helplessness..."
     —WS from EDM

While *Pater Noster* blazed away above
Cell blocks in Hartford, he would turn the dial
And scan eclectic spaces of his mind
For airings of a more dissenting style.
Deaf-eared to channels wooing from the past
He'd sound electric pipelines like the blind
Until seditions took the place at last
Of all illusions crooned to toys of time.

Perhaps a vision came of Heraclitus
A fireball packed with rabbits in his hand
Dispersing from his hot magician's hat
Menageries to fertilize the land,
While farther off he saw our father raze
His daughters, sons, the search, each novel phrase.

Love's Legacy

Still Abraham, with ready blade
Prepares the altar, hangs the vine
Each season with new fruit to quench
Earth's thirst for sacrificial wine.

Executor of nature's will,
He serves the sod, must till and bring
With every celebrated birth
His ancient lord an offering:

His ripened yield, the precious fruit
Half-shrunken back to seed in time
Yet one more wrathful vintage crushed
By rote transitions of the clime.

Heeding the Prophet

He warns the keg's about to blow
Unless they do as he's suggested.
In view of those who run the show,
Perhaps his theory should be tested.

The Marionette Show

Back on his business, the king's men come
In search of a role, a stint with the leery,
A ticket to pipedreams, new means when they're done
To breathe hallowed air and seldom grow weary.
He jockeys them well, their coarse, grainy lord,
A puppeteer whisking them to and fro
From treasuries tapped, to divine reward,
Sweet pinches of salt burned after each show.

His slaves labor hard, and play a part too,
Sometimes so eager to please and suffice
It enters your head that it might be you
They are seeking, and not their true love's price,
You even who might be pulling the strings—
As if one could rival the king of kings.

Letting in the Draft

Like birds, my friend, our goose will soon be cooked
And there'll be little else to hold our view;
There's prob'lly somewhere else that someone's looked
But I have no idea where or who.
I know it's not myself who's speaking now,
It must be he who comes on certain nights
And gives me something special to endow
The reading public with, on their rare flights.
It's . . . well, like leaving earth a while and then,
Far out among the visions one beholds . . .
Just . . . letting you be you, or just pretend
You weren't in sight of all the constant scolds.
It has its way of making one content.
I'm not so much a rebel as a gent.

Regardless

Although what comes tomorrow
   Cannot be told today,
A change of weather's likely
   And always on the way;

And where no clouds are noted
   Nor shadows seen about,
The rain will fall regardless,
   When all our luck runs out.

On the Urgency of Replenishing the Workforce

When all earth's paths are bound to double back
Upon themselves, no matter what we do,
It somehow seems mere critical presumption
To be demanding anything of you
As if one bore more claim to any right.
The fly is on the wheel, and we are on it,
All brought around in time, to something black,
Dumb and unknowing, cured of every zeal,
The race's bluster, and all pride of reason.
Enough to bear with that, to where it leads
Without a superadded servitude.
No wonder some slip harness and secede,
Go snatching wages where and how they dare,
Then fling them cavalierly in the air.

A Brief Alarm

Like everything, this too will soon be lost,
Forever out of sight and out of mind,
A brief alarm resorbed into the sum
Of passing things that leave no trace behind.
For its duration, it would summon all
To a restraint heroic—to be brave
Beyond all generations gone before,
And make a sacrifice more sure to save:

To starve the ground, and lay no further feast
For bloated Earth's unflagging appetite,
But be content to plow redemptively
A barren field in which no seed seeks light
And make your plots the last wherein to toss
A harvest raised for neverending loss.

Chapeau Bouquet

Magic lovers longed for more
From seedlings sprung in restive hours,

Some hint of happy times in store,
A forecast bright as springtime flowers.

He hatched them in his hat at night,
Companions courted to advance

The time, but struck by chilling light
They withered like a failed romance.

A Demurral

Why keep your senses grounded here,
Or let them have you sharp and clear

Who wakened you to numbered days
To yoke you to their futile ways?

While tickings winch you nearer toward
Your execution and reward,

Why not imbibe—or pick your trip,
Let them ram home the standard script

As you, absorbing what you like
Risk transport on a one-way flight;

Let our grand architects complain,
Who pull their mighty weight in vain,

Only to end as they began,
Fragile freight of a circling hand

That flicks the feeble out and in
And each back to his origin.

Quoth the Raven from the Ballroom Bar

Neither the understanding of the dead
nor that of the living, can ever be enough,
can ever be more

than a sort of dark familiar, say
which, when perched on your belly at night
often speaks to you when you gaze

through its locked obsidian eyes
and see a kind of chronic
malady of mind,

an inescapable vision reverting
again and again to life's bright harvest,
the permanent absence ahead,

and you sense at the core a sort of shocked
apprehension of being's essential neverness,
of the blot-out factor in the blood,

at least until an indifferently riddling
tongue begins to block your thinking,
and you start sinking

down toward desired oblivion,
down toward the ocean's nightbound floor,
where seeing hopefully is done.

There really is nothing more
to share than this ultimate understanding
of organic fact, the process of decay,

innate corruptibility and the gradual
breakdown of all that seemed solid
and real. And yet, notwithstanding,

it's a ball, an opera, a bar—your due
and fully owed ration of every sought thrill
though it's still,

though none of it ever really happened,
just whatever happens to you.

Bypassing the Mill

Man added to our last reward the torture
Of doing things one hates, on old death row—
And as grape turns to raisin in the scorcher,
Aghast his slaves all face where they must go.
Condemned though innocent, one serves one's time
Because...because—it seems the only choice?
And while the world mechanically wheels by,
One does what seems required with muted voice.
Yet there are those who do not bear the yoke,
But find a way around the rote ordeal—
Who let sweet *Chemineaud* and the odd toke
Command their hours and get them primed to feel,
Who if they waste in some half-snuffed Gomorrah,
Still let Old Faithful spout and tend the flora.

Frequent Flyer Program

Life sometimes seems like slower suicide,
Since taking happy flights is half what kills:
The fuel consumed, the surge and beat past dawn
Of countless re-accelerated thrills.
Still, why put off all flying stunts till heaven
When now or never's when to claim your due—
With yeast to hand, and Sodom yet uncrushed
Why not let geysers gush in Xanadu?

Embarrassment abates inside a cloud,
Where blushing selves more freely join the act—
Sworn tipplers lose and find themselves in fog,
With other trippers who steer off the track.
Some say it's best to live before you die,
And silent choirs of angels all know why.

Scattered Ashes

A self was strewn like appleseed
    Across the newmown hay;
From sleep to sleep no cry availed,
    So still the grasses lay.

All end, I knew, as things bestrewn
    Like shells across a shore,
Each emptied vessel borne alone
    To sands of nevermore.

Yet shells are full of distant winds,
    Strange voices in the void—
O long I searched a shore of shells
    For love yet undestroyed.

But when I laid my head to rest
    Down near a slow, slow sea,
Only the sand, heard clear as sleep
    Lay breathing next to me.

Shock Therapy

What's left to do
now you're no longer you,
when whatever you say
goes the opposite way
till one's driven as always
to doors slammed on hallways
then relief one's alone
in a hostage-freed zone;

except call off all bets,
be untorn by regrets,
once again one's heart's master
as progressively after
enough numbing swindles
no fond thought rekindles
that old wish you'll come back
now you're no one I lack.

Death in Life

Though his demise was not like that
Of billions lodged beneath the ground,
Yet it was cast as such to one
Who must believe him buried now.
It helped sidestep analysis
Of faith's demolishment by phone,
And rendered pointless idle queries
About affairs no longer known.
Should he be spotted on some *rue*
Not visibly yet void of breath,
That hunched ghost shinning into view
Might but recall his sudden death,
The funeral held, the obit quoted,
And down an aisle a coffin toted.

Huit Clos

Shut in by spirits blocking all
   Escape in sounds or sights,
Their prisoner stares at endless days,
   Nor finds release in nights;

His mind so sealed within its bone,
   So hopeless to uncage,
Not even sleep will come to turn
   A mute, unspeaking page.

Diluvian Meditation

More and more, as he kept tracking new
Awakenings of flesh, and nothing served
To ease the pained awareness out of mind,
He feared his final bill for life was due.
As rivers trespass fields in a flood,
Defy containment, spill their banks and run
To regions rarely focused on, so spread
Such poisons as men nurture in their blood.

Though apprehensive, he resolved to wait,
Content to ply his pleas as antidote
And hope a miracle might detour fate,
And while odd feelings preyed upon his peace
Supposed, if something had him by the throat,
This way or that, sensation yet would cease.

On a Proposed New Course

It's said they keep their distance, perhaps are
Vainly cryptic, for all their humble prose,
And no close kin to any erstwhile master.

*Well surely it's not everyone who knows
To tune his lyre to a living ear.*
Some find their vaunted taste for our true tongue

Belied by phrases ringing less familiar
Than those of those we daily prate among.
The outworn ousted way was out of touch.

*These birthed a lingo nearer to our own,
Clipped clean of artifice and with a much
More earthy lean.*

   —Sweet secrets wrapped in loam!—
A full house, then, will be assured, of course?
What native could not wish to master Morse?

Officially Speaking

What nugget gleaned may we bestow
To mark the passing of the torch
Who watch the darkness watch us go
Steaming across a lamp-lit porch.
A few steps off our haloed stage
The boundless night with sealed lips
Counts out the customary wage:
An ineluctable eclipse.

It comes to us in daily thought
And haunts us every day we breathe,
How we without a hope have sought
To love where we could only grieve
And only honed a skill so wise
To take a sage to his demise.

Revenge of the Clock

In dark times before,
full of bore after bore,
   into what have the bored ones
      descended?

Such off-beat pursuits
as leather and boots?
   Or were poppy-seed dreams
      recommended?

Perhaps to defeat
ennui and the creep
   of the clock, a fine art
      was befriended—

And pates duly seeded,
creation proceeded,
   while unnoticed, days darkened
      and ended—

But whatever solution
brought diminution
   of a dead-weight of hours,
      time—offended—

Avenged every trick
to slip its slow tick,
   and ran out, because left
      unattended!

Departure

Well boxed, and neatly packaged like a thing,
Back from the final purge he duly came,
The pulverized reduction postmen bring
When bodies have become cold feast for flame.
Into a vessel made to store the crushed
I poured the coarse remains of someone fine—
A bag of bits, of gray and grainy dust,
One shocking essence spirit leaves behind.
Housed now in hard cement beneath the ground,
He cannot share the living's deep concerns,
Nor must he yet endure, unsafe, unsound
As we who tremble while we wait our turns.
Behind him lies the pain past all relief,
The love that yet makes good its threat of grief.

An Ideal Substitution

Erase, erase, erase—call up a blank,
Let nothing be where nothing was before,
A nothing that seemed something—only see,
Behind your eye, some piece of dead decor.
Empty your head of haunters, wring and wring
Desire's root until you squeeze it dry,
Gorge on ideals, till bored by everything,
Lapsed and replete, your mind is free to die.

Ever and always singing their old tune:
"You won't be disappointed, O you'll see!
Back and back we'll all be coming soon,
Prepare yourself for promised ecstasy"—
And onward ticks the clock, and no one knocks.
Time to review some ancient mental buttocks.

Excerpt from Hamlet's Diary

Some life-pulse agitates the stars
    Tonight, and breaks their spell,
As memory stirs in beamless eyes,
    Or depths move in a well.

Secluded in a nave, one light
    In private tempest throws
Fierce shadow-struggle over walls
    Some secret ghost-wind blows.

And sunken embers, ashen-faced
    Flare suddenly unstirred,
And through the timbered hush, a gulp
    From some lone pond is heard.

Time's watch lives on, a brooding lull
    Disguising depths aroused;
Sleep, of remembrance is not quit,
    And spirits walk unhoused.

In the Stillness of Many

Many nights when undrawn to the living,
    I have gone to the graveyard instead,
And sought out my truth among ashes,
    And for beauty, lain down with the dead.

In the stillness of many a midnight,
    I have warmed to their wakening sound,
The impassioned, and scorned, and unliving
    Who speak to my heart from the ground.

Tomorrow Some New Star

Upon the stars tonight appears some care,
Some stricken pulse, as blurs the silent pool
Or wavers in some ancient's vacant stare;
Say they were borne there by a love proved cruel,

Drawn as by some brute hypnotic power
Out into fields of deep night's lonely hell;
As vigil lights are wrenched in their low hour,
Something not yet lulled by time's dim spell

Seems waked in them; which heart's fresh longings
Rise tonight, and reach up there to wring
Perhaps some life from those emerging eyes
So almost moved in their frail glimmering?

Tomorrow some new star must yearn, as when
One heart grows still, and one turns blind to men.

Madame LaBouche

Her ears pricked up so much, *Madame
LaBouche*, decrying all disturbance
Insisted sounds around be less
City-like and more suburban.

One bistro gave *Madame* no rest
Until it was at last subdued,
And vexed by yakky cabbies next,
She finally got their stand removed.

Yet still, some night-owl might abort
The dreamshift of *LaBouche's* week,
And pop her prized unconsciousness
By passing with a piercing shriek,

Or other nuisances emerge—
But when, for my part, out a window
I spot *Madame* surveying things,
Hard eye a-gleam, arms set akimbo

All poised to nail some passerby
With shrill bursts from her magic flute—
I see the sole noisemaker I
Have lately dreamed of going mute.

Song of the Alley Cat

O give me a bottle
And let me forget
All of this struggle
And passion to get;

Presume no desire
To pull in the fight;
O give me a bottle,
And bid me goodnight.

Urban Fare

Stranger than anyone he sits
in gravel lot with food in hand
in kitchen chair set up with four
chrome legs, a seat, a backrest, and

eating his supper there alone
amid jalopies, litter, dust
and tar-patched backsides of sweet homes
lived in by ones few bankers trust

he thinks, typewriting at his corn,
the summer stillness of the scene,
ruptured by scream and screech and horn
might well as not be briefly seen.

A Hoot for the Labor League

They knew no reason to secede,
Those village criers, smooth or rough
Whose industry-abetting words
Did not suspect clear nights enough,
Nor note in starry midnight's shimmer
A dead-eye's homicidal glimmer
Observed when staring into space
Before the witness is erased.

US in Them

The long neglected park now blooms,
Is groomed, subdued; its tame affairs
Kept bland by badgering patrols
Who promenade the streets in pairs.
The shift appears about complete,
From hub of local untaxed trade
To guarded garden spot reserved
For workers less covertly paid.
Cyclists wheeling in at night
In search of rebel remnants scan
The iron-fenced perimeter,
But beams disclose a vacant land,
Beachhead secure from blade to bough,
A strong south wind prevailing now.

Cell Theory

Where they now go to catch a wink
Who stretched out on the green before
Or made hard benches beds because
They lacked a key to any door,
Who knows, but parks gone tenantless
And prisons crammed and overfull
Suggest how sudden aesthetes made
The local scene so wonderful.
Fat tabs for sleeping out of doors
Collectible in cash or time
Now equal several millions owed
La ville by ones without a dime,
And jail for all nonpaying guests
Keeps flowerpaths more picturesque.

Palmistry in Paradise

Strange, how in the park today,
Three wheeled around on me and one
Required the reason I was there;
No doubt some wondered what I'd done,
As I, best as I could impaired
By lips gone gummy with alarm,
In forced defense invoked the plot's
Exclusive new Edenic charm.
Directed— "for our safety"—next
To show my palms, I did; and then,
"We want no more dead bodies here,"
Said he, who may, to weed out men
Check lifelines of all comers who
Resemble him he said I do.

Reactionary Phase

In martial mode they pass and pass,
On bicycles, in cars, on foot,
Relentlessly parading proof
Old laissez-faire has gone kaput.
But strategy grows more refined:
Compounding tensions on the rise,
In unaccustomed spots appear
Sly pairs positioned to surprise.
You had supposed yourself alone,
When something then still out of view
Was poised to startle your repose.
Seated on a park bench two
The other day—I felt their eyes—
Tracked traffic in New Paradise.

Square Times Blues

The only show in town shut down,
Dispatched to some unknown address,
A leafy peace has settled in
Where none had come to convalesce.
Le carnaval, for all those tricks
Condignly sampled on the cheap,
Still leavened with expectancy
A long day's journey into sleep.
Perhaps in some unpurged locale
Yet free for all to occupy,
Our banished horde of hawkers hail
And hook such gamer passersby
As we who, undeprived had plied
A city not yet countrified.

Preparing for the Pageant

Our tiny central park transformed,
Renewed, its state-appointed heirs
On brighter workdays come at noon
To claim the space an hour as theirs.
Few, of the once emboldened who
Had plied a seedy green unchecked,
Now brave the odds and navigate
The precincts of the New Elect.
Unleashed by some contestant's dream,
Wry rovers licensed to coerce
Compliance, hound and hold them back,
While I, who watch the tide reverse,
See, where the undisturbed now tarry
A pretty city cemetery.

Advice for Winston

Why not just impose the old Zurich curfew,
drive everyone indoors early, arrest
anyone caught in the street past eleven.

Surely that would bring to an end
all disapproved transactions
conducted in the blind of night

as well as providing a superabundance
of quietude, a lullaby
for the fierce upholders of right.

Maybe you've never been approached
by someone peddling forbidden fruit
and felt glad the option was there,

but far better they, any day, I'd say
than heaven's unleashed hounds
accosting anyone they please

with gratuitous curiosities.
Do you really want to live that way?
And now with all the good people

being asked to spy on everyone else
and supplement the force, Winston,
make yourself thin, shrink

out of the screen's wide eye,
it's a quarter century ago,
and so,

1984, here we come.

Between Frosts

Framed in my front slider now,
maples masquerading as giant
forsythias in full bloom
will very soon be revealing how
an early leaf's a short-lived flower.

But greater than any loss I prevision
in April's fleeting golden hour
is a building promise of release
from another eternal winter's prison,
wide-open doors and the long-awaited

warm luxurious freedom of being
part of the scene again, at least
till its culminant powers unfold a final
tapestry made to fade away . . .
in earth's perennial pageant of decay.

Then Pines

How spring's first green is gold
   The not yet weeping
Willows show,
   When in the sketch called April, they
Like faint forsythias glow.

Then pines,
   Like men who must endure
Though all their treasure pass,
   Mark summer's end where fall's first change
Lies golden in the grass.

Pronounced and Deep

Pronounced and deep it was,
   The feeling of that day
When distant years were missed
   And seemed so far away;

O autumn tears it was,
   And sobbing fits in spring,
But not so deep as now,
   When loss is everything.

Blessing the Cup

While morning yet was rose, not thorn,
Earth glistening as if newly born,
I came across a romance here:
He hadn't seen the shadows clear,
Nor seemed to be at all aware;
She watched, and was content to stare.

I thought of how a love began,
Of Eden, too, the dawn of man
And how that garden turned to grief;
Of sorrow borne without relief;
And yet, I did not fail to bless
The tainted cup of happiness,
Nor reverently to tiptoe by
This sleeper in the flower's eye.

Companions

Composing the flock I thought I heard
   When wonder drew me out the door,
A solitary mockingbird,
   Busily being more,

Absorbed in his little crowd of sounds,
   A parody of me,
Was gathering in his singleness
   Some songs for company.

Adventure Beckons

Adventure beckons everywhere
To any child at heart;

Creation, just by being there,
Precludes a life apart.

Undimmed within by souls grown old
They never lose the world,

That oyster with its magic hold,
For them forever pearled.

Personal Exemption

Though almost every time he spoke
His nose was sure to grow,
Truth's beauty did not much concern
Our Old Pinocchio—

Except in love, where pugs were all
And unequivocally
He'd warn each passing schoolgirl crush:
Just never lie to me!

ee cummings

some say ee cummings had a poets soul
loved his motherfather (wifefriends) could write
most beautifully (if always on the whole
not as those with higher eyes and oes might;
but then it was lamented sorely by
a few at harvard at the time that all
the best poems had been written;so why
try to climb old mountains but to fall
(having etched short of the supreme engrav (e)
ing) back into a crumpled ball;and why not
try hand at some quite unbeforedone (brave
thing) and outjink the comparative blot
of shakespeare shelley byron moore hood keats
and leave them towering high; in
(old) dead beats

A Minor Croak

I hear them trilling bird songs to each other
In the cherry blossom climate
Of togetherness.
Pigeons on the roof
Seem to parody this pair—
But they will go
With the wandering summer ease of lovers
Along the river's turns, and I—
I can only feel very
Like a frog held captive in a columbary.

After the Hurricane
(Cape Cod, Summer '91)

If only this lost gold were all
   The beauty not to be,
And leaves in August raining brown
   From every stormstruck tree

Were all the treasure stripped away
   From helpless arms too early,
And every lovely season lost
   Were coming back as surely.

Consolation for the Disenchanted

Time will stop
And death will come;
All will perish,
Fade,
Be done.

Why complain then?
Drink!
Be merry!
Life—
Is only temporary.

Summer Yardwork

I seek no gift of song today,
  No melody self-made,
But something hard and uninspired,
  To draw the chilling shade.

Doubtless sleep would better serve
  To rouse them from their lairs,
And make the stealthy shadows come
  And take me unawares.

But in this blind and watchful mood,
  Which stalls the flow of time,
Since dreams are far, I move the sun
  By wrestling out a rhyme.

Canadian Club vs. Catechism Class

Can it be me?
Or is it by chance
That whenever I sing
There's no one to dance?
(I might as well put
The whole world in a trance.)

With my opulent view
Am I so out of touch?
Too far out of sync?
Not normal enough?
Are my sparkling *bijoux*
Just a little too much?

Going with the Flow

Pick for yourself
something you'd like;
let it be deep
or guiltily light;

let it have rhythm,
let it be sad,
let it be happy,
let it be mad.

Who really cares
if it's any of those;
you might as well stick
to conversing in prose;

you might as well say
what they'd all like to hear:
how it's good, really good
that we all landed here

where nature's best laws
backed by church and by state
keep dispatching fresh ranks
toward a heavenly fate.

Auscultation

Inside oneself one sounds all parts:
A vague suspension of the breeze,

A rift between raw pulp and clime
The first frost of the meta-freeze.

A rugged oarsman's heave and pull
Keeps muffled drumming audible,

Mind mindful of an aural whir
Like summer nightfall's teeming chirr,

Of ice, locked hinges, treacheries,
Cold timbers groaning on high seas.

Such Things Must Draw

Cathedral hush at twilight hour
   In Junes spent long ago,
Stray crickets blurting out their song,
   The grass scent, and the glow

Of fireflies sparking dusk-filled air
   Whose dense and deepening hue
Nightfall would overtake too fast—
   Such things must draw now, too,

And still those potent stars must rise,
   The prayer that skies be fair,
As when, on evenings thought of now,
   I thrilled to breathe June air.

Love Came a Second Time

Love came a second time, but I
   Could hardly use my tongue;
It came to me when life was sore,
   And I could not be young.

It was as if a sudden sun
   Had blown the star-vault bright;
A match struck in a cavern—then
   An avalanche of night.

And so, as in a sleep I went,
   Eyes open but to mind,
To find below the verge, a sun
   That long had ceased to shine.

Brighter Are All

Brighter are all the greens of June
   When rains have washed them clean,
Than in the sunshine's gauzy glow,
   When radiance pales the scene;

Pure as the tear-bright cheek for which
   We beg the clouds to part
And banish beauty so extreme
   It conquers the proud heart.

Into the Winter Clad

Into the winter clad the great
   And lovely pinetrees go;
When all that made them sing has flown,
   Some meet the season so.

No numb display for ones they held
   When arms were filled with feather;
But maples strip themselves and wait
   The balm of bitter weather.

Once

In springtime, once, May's thrill became
    Tears mourning things gone by;
October, too, distilled such mist,
    For love unwrung from high.

And summer, once, could stir the child
    With dreams of brighter days,
And even winter surely held
    Allure of younger ways.

But now, the seasons glow and fade,
    Less shades of ache or joy;
And as the world goes by, I miss
    Once longing for the boy.

By Land or By Sea

Away from the ever-dragging chain
   Of human industry,
I sought a lonely beach to breathe
   The spirit of the sea.

And in and in and in they roll,
   Lumbering toward the land,
To cast their burdens down and go,
   As froth runs off the sand.

Outlaw's Retreat

It runs through the yellowed,
  unblown leaves,
    where listening
      has rewards:

Sweet stream
  of banished melodies
  whose song
    I hasten towards.

About Tom Merrill

Ever since a lucky tip led him almost a decade ago to *The Hypertexts*, an online poetry publisher that proved entirely hospitable to his writing, Tom's poetry, with few exceptions besides the occasional book opportunity like this one, has been published only on the internet.

Time in Eternity represents the third such opportunity to come his way in the past eight years. It follows close on the heels of *Facing The Remains*, a perceptively assembled sampling of his poetry brought out by exotbooks in NYC in 2012 and available at the publisher's website along with other handsomely produced chapbooks in the exotbooks poetry series. The firstborn of the lucky trio of collections, *Outlaw's Retreat*, was sponsored by *The Hypertexts* and published in 2005 by Multicultural Books in Richmond, British Columbia. Reviews of Tom's books are available at *The Hypertexts* website.

Two earlier titles by Tom are *Inside Out* and *Once Scenes*, the first a poetry collection, the other a mixed-media production comprised of his photography, painting and poetry that was conceived as a commemoration of the 9/11 tragedy. An excerpt and several photos from the latter can be found on his poetry page at *The Hypertexts*.

As well as having been published in numerous poetry journals, he has judged a number of poetry contests, and back when he was still appearing in magazines, even managed to snag a trophy every now and then in such contests himself.

One of his poems was recently published by THE UNITED NATIONS International Public Policy Institute, and a couple of others by The Voices Project, and a number of his poems have been translated into foreign languages. And within just the past few months, a little string of his poems appeared in successive editions of a newspaper for the homeless in Tennessee.

He was named *Poet in Residuum* at *The Hypertexts* in 2008, and has served as an Advisory Editor there ever since.

www.ingramcontent.com/pod-product-compliance
Lightning Source LLC
Chambersburg PA
CBHW070303100426
42743CB00011B/2327